THE STORY OF JESUS

CHRISTOPHER DOYLE
AND
GILLIAN CHAPMAN

Contents

A very special mother

Jesus had a mother called Mary. It was a bit of a surprise to her to be told that she would be the mother of such an important baby. It happened like this.

One day Mary was sitting by herself. Suddenly she saw one of God's messengers. The angel Gabriel just appeared in front of her.

'Peace to you, Mary,' said Gabriel, gently. 'The Lord has blessed you.'

Now, it isn't every day an angel visits you. Mary didn't know what to say. In fact she was quite worried. She wondered what the angel could mean.

'Don't be afraid, Mary,' Gabriel reassured her. 'God has chosen you to be the mother of a special child. When he is born you are to call him Jesus. He will be a king and his holy kingdom will never come to an end.'

'But how can I have a son?' Mary asked. 'I haven't even a husband. I'm not ready to start a

family yet,' she said.

'God's special helper, the Holy Spirit, will make this happen,' explained the angel. 'Jesus will be the Son of God himself.'

Mary saw then how important this job was.

She looked down and said quietly, 'I am the servant of the Lord. I am ready to do whatever God wants of me.'

Jesus is born

Joseph had been engaged to Mary for a while. The angel Gabriel spoke to Joseph in a dream, telling him to marry her now.

Some months later, Mary and Joseph travelled together to Bethlehem to be counted in the census. The Roman Emperor who ruled their country wanted to know how many people lived there so he could collect taxes from them.

When they arrived in the town they

found that there was nowhere to stay; all the rooms had already been taken. Only one kind innkeeper offered them room – and that was in a stable with the animals.

That night Mary's baby was born. Gently she wrapped him in special clothes. She put him down in a manger full of hay.

On a hillside outside the town there were some shepherds looking after their sheep. They huddled together to keep warm. As they dozed, a dazzling light shone all around them. The angel Gabriel appeared in front of them, and they were afraid.

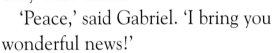

'Peace,' said Gabriel. 'I bring you wonderful news!'

'What's he talking about?' muttered the shepherds.

'Tonight a special baby was born,' announced the angel. 'He is the king you have been waiting for, God's Saviour. To see him you must go to Bethlehem where you will find him lying in a manger.'

Suddenly there were hundreds more angels, singing, 'Glory to God in the highest, and peace to his people on earth!'

The shepherds rubbed their eyes in amazement, then set off at once to see the new king.

Some important visitors

Some time after Jesus was born, Mary received some unusual visitors. Some important men travelled a long way from the east.

They had followed a strange new star in the sky that seemed to move ahead of them. Their books had told them that the star was the sign of a very special birth – the birth of a king!

The star brought them first to Jerusalem, the most important city in Israel. They thought this was the place to find a new king. But when they went to the royal palace, Jesus wasn't there. King Herod sent them

to Bethlehem, but he was anxious about the new king. Surely no one could take his place, he thought?

The men set off again to Bethlehem where they found Jesus, with his mother Mary. The men unloaded their camels and presented their gifts to Jesus.

'I bring gold, fit for a king,' said the first.

'My gift is frankincense, for this boy will grow to be a priest as well,' said the second.

The third opened a jar containing myrrh. 'This sweet smelling spice points to his future death, for when this boy grows up, he must die because of what he says and does.'

These were very expensive gifts to give to a baby. Mary wasn't sure what to make of it all. She thought about it a great deal and wondered what these visitors could mean.

Then the wise men set off to travel back to their own country, having been warned by God in a dream, not to go back to King Herod.

Jesus goes missing

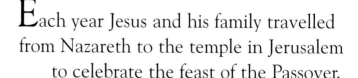

Each year Jesus and his family travelled from Nazareth to the temple in Jerusalem to celebrate the feast of the Passover.

One year, when Jesus was twelve years old, Mary and Joseph set off for home at the end of the feast with all the other people they had travelled with. They guessed Jesus was with other members of the family or friends. At the end of the first day's journey, Mary was preparing their evening meal.

'Joseph,' she said to her husband, 'go and see if you can find Jesus. He must be hungry by now.'

Joseph asked around. 'Has anyone here seen Jesus?'

'No, he's not with us,' some of them said. 'In fact we haven't seen him all day.'

Mary and Joseph began to worry. Where could Jesus be? They travelled back to Jerusalem and searched high and low for him. After three days they were becoming desperate. Finally they went to the temple again for one last look. To their amazement they

found Jesus sitting with the teachers, listening to them and asking questions. He seemed to understand everything they were saying.

'Why have you upset us like this, son?' asked Mary, anxiously. 'We've been so worried about you.'

'You shouldn't have worried,' replied Jesus. 'Didn't you know that I must be in my Father's house?'

Mary and Joseph didn't know what to say to this; they didn't understand what he meant. So Jesus went back home with them. He grew taller and stronger and always obeyed his parents. But Mary wondered about what the wise men had said at his birth.

13

Jesus is baptised

Before Jesus was born, his mother had visited her relative, Elizabeth, and found that she was also going to have a baby. Her son, John, was now grown up, as Jesus was.

John lived in the desert, and ate wild honey and locusts; he wore a cloth made out of camel's hair with a leather belt around his waist.

'Repent!' he called out. 'Say sorry and ask God to forgive you for your bad ways. Come into the water as a sign that your sins have been washed away.'

Many people came to the River Jordan to be baptised.

'You will see someone soon who is much more important than I am,' said John. 'He is so important I wouldn't even feel able to untie his sandals.'

The people wondered who he was talking about.

Then, one day, Jesus came to the river to be baptised too. John recognised him straight away.

'I shouldn't be baptising you,' John said. 'You should baptise me!'

'Let's do it anyway,' replied Jesus. So John baptised him.

As Jesus stood up out of the water, the sky seemed to open. Then what looked like a dove fluttered down and rested on him. The people who were watching heard a voice.

'This is my Son. I love him and am pleased with him.'

This was a sign from God that Jesus should begin the work he was sent to do.

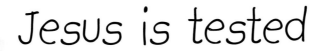

Jesus is tested

After his baptism, Jesus went into the desert. He didn't eat for forty days and nights. He was very hungry. It was then the devil chose to test Jesus.

'If you are God's Son, why not turn these stones into bread to eat?' said the devil.

'People don't live just on bread; they must also live by what God teaches', replied Jesus.

The devil then carried Jesus to the top of the highest tower on the temple.

'Throw yourself off this tower; don't the scriptures say that God will order his angels to catch you?'

Jesus replied again, 'They also say that you should not put God to the test.'

The devil tried one last time to catch him out. He took Jesus to the top of a high mountain. The land stretched out all round as far as the eye could see.

'I'll give you all this,' said the devil, 'if you will just kneel down and worship me.'

Jesus turned to the devil and, using his name, spoke sternly.

'Get away from me, Satan. I won't kneel before you. The scriptures say that you should worship God and him alone.'

Then the devil left and angels came to help Jesus as he prepared for his work.

15

The huge catch of fish

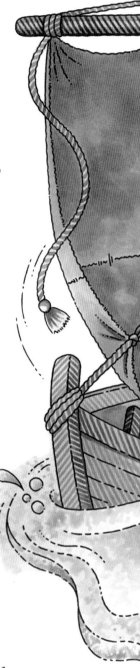

Jesus walked down by the lake in Galilee. Many people were jostling to see him. Jesus looked around and saw two fishing boats left by some fishermen while they washed their nets.

'May I get into your boat?' asked Jesus. 'That way I can talk to these people more easily.'

So Simon and his brother, Andrew, pushed the boat a little way out. When he had finished speaking, Jesus turned to Simon.

'Why don't you take us into the deeper water? Let down your nets and see what we can catch.'

'We were out all last night but didn't catch anything,' Simon protested. 'But if you think it's worth it, we'll try.'

So Simon and Andrew cast their nets into the water. To their surprise they caught hundreds of fish. When they tried to haul them in, the net started to tear.

'Quickly,' called Simon to his partners, 'come and help us land this catch.'

James and John sailed out and the fishermen loaded the fish between the two boats. The catch was so heavy that both boats started to sink. Simon was amazed. He fell on his knees in front of Jesus.

'You must go away from me,' he said. 'I am not a good man.'

'Don't be afraid,' said Jesus. 'From now on I want you to follow me and catch people for God.'

With that, Simon, Andrew, James and John left their fishing business and followed Jesus.

They were the first of twelve men altogether whom Jesus called to be his special friends.

God cares about you

One day Jesus was teaching a large crowd. He told them many things about God that they hadn't realised before. He then turned to his disciples to teach them these truths also.

'Don't worry about what you will eat or what you will wear. Life is more important than that.

'Think about the birds flying around us. They don't sow seeds or harvest grain. They don't store the harvest in barns, do they? No, God gives them food to eat when they need it. If he thinks that much of them, think how much more important you are to him.'

Jesus then asked them a question.

'How many of you can add years to your life just by thinking about it? Well, if you can't do that, why worry about other things? Look at the wild flowers growing in the fields. They are dressed more beautifully even than King Solomon in his best robes.

'God cares about you,' Jesus told them. 'You matter to him. God even knows how many hairs there are on your head.

'Don't worry about what you need to eat and drink. Think about what you need to do to be part of God's kingdom and do that. God will then give you everything you need as well.'

A desperate man

A man once came to Jesus asking to be healed.

The other people kept away. They had been taught never to go near a person suffering from leprosy. It was a dangerous skin disease. You could catch it by touching someone already ill.

The man was desperate. He threw himself on the ground in front of Jesus.

'I know you can help me if you want to. Please make me clean,' he pleaded.

Jesus looked at the man with pity.

'I do want to help you,' said Jesus as he stretched out his hand and actually touched the man. 'Be clean.'

In an instant, the man's damaged skin became smooth; he was healed.

Now, in those days, when someone recovered from leprosy there were laws they were supposed to follow. Jesus reminded the man about this.

'Go and show yourself to the priest, then offer the sacrifice that Moses ordered,' Jesus told him. 'And by the way, don't tell anyone

what has happened here today.'

But the man was so happy, he had to tell as many people as he could. Soon the news had spread far and wide. Many people came to see Jesus and asked him to help them too.

Whenever Jesus wanted some time alone to pray, he had to go off by himself into the lonely desert.

A hole in the roof

When Jesus returned to Capernaum, many people came to him to be healed. The religious leaders known as Pharisees and other teachers of the law had also come to hear what Jesus had to say. The house where Jesus was teaching was packed.

Outside, some men struggled as they carried their friend on his bed. He couldn't walk or even sit up. The friends were sure Jesus could help him. But when they arrived and saw the crowds blocking the doorway, the men could see no way in.

'I know,' said one. 'Let's go up on the roof.'

The men clambered up the steps at the side of the house. They started pulling apart the mud and branches that made up the roof. When the hole was big enough, they lowered their friend down into the room where Jesus was.

Jesus saw how much faith they had and

he turned to the man on the bed.

'My friend, your sins are forgiven.'

The Pharisees and teachers started muttering.

'How can he say that? Only God can forgive sins.'

'What is easier for me to say: "Your sins are forgiven," or "Get up and walk"?' Without waiting for an answer, Jesus turned back to the man and said, 'Up you get. Take your bed home with you.'

The man stood up for the first time in years. He picked up his bed and walked out, thanking God for his cure.

'How wonderful!' the people cried. 'It's amazing!'

Jesus had healed the man. He had also shown the Pharisees and teachers of the law that he had the power to forgive sins.

The healing at the pool

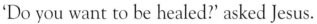

Near the Sheep Gate in Jerusalem there was a pool surrounded by archways. When the water bubbled it was said that the first person to step into the pool would be healed.

There were many people lying around the pool. Many of them were there every day and had been ill for a long time. Jesus spoke to one man who had been ill for thirty-eight years.

'Do you want to be healed?' asked Jesus.

'There's no one here to help me,' the man answered. 'Every time the water bubbles someone else gets in before I can move.'

'You don't need to worry about that any more,' said Jesus. 'Pick up your mat and walk.'

The man didn't wait to be told twice. The water hadn't bubbled; no one had helped him stand. But he stood up and walked. Jesus had made him well.

24

Jesus calms a storm

Jesus' friends always seemed to be learning something new about him.

'Let's sail the boat over to the other side of the lake,' he said to them after he had been busy healing people all day.

So they pushed the boat into the water. When they set off, the weather was fine. The lapping of the waves in the breeze was so peaceful that Jesus lay down in the boat and fell fast asleep.

Suddenly, from nowhere, a storm swept down the lake. The waves rose and the wind lashed at the sail and the ropes. Things became so bad that the boat started to fill with water. Now, some of Jesus' friends were good

sailors, but even they were afraid that the boat might sink.

'Jesus! Wake up!' they cried. 'We're all going to drown.'

Jesus stood up in the boat. Calmly, he stretched out his hand and said simply, 'Peace. Be still.'

With that, the wind died down and the waves became just small ripples on the surface of the water. He turned to his friends.

'Why were you afraid?' he said. 'Where is your faith?'

The men were amazed.

'Who is this man?' they said to each other. 'How is it that he has such power that even the wind and waves do as he tells them?'

Jesus heals a little girl

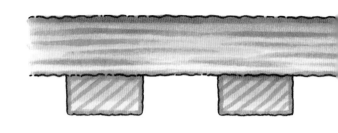

People were waiting for Jesus when he came back across the lake. As he was walking through the crowd, a Jewish official called Jairus knelt in front of him.

'My twelve-year-old daughter is seriously ill,' wailed Jairus. 'Please come to my house – I know you can heal her.'

Jesus agreed and began to follow Jairus to his home. But while he was walking the crowd were jostling and pushing him. Suddenly he stopped.

'Who touched me then?' asked Jesus.

Everyone around thought this a strange thing to say: there were so many people touching him. Then an old lady came forward.

'I have been bleeding for twelve years. No doctors can heal me. I knew if I could just touch the hem of your cloak it could make me well again.'

Jesus looked at her kindly. 'Your faith has healed you. Go in peace,' he said.

At that moment one of the servants from Jairus' house rushed up.

'Don't bother the master any more. Your daughter has just died.'

But Jesus ignored the servant.

'Don't be afraid,' said Jesus. 'She is just sleeping.' And he set off for Jairus' house.

When he arrived he took in with him Peter, John and James and the little girl's parents. Jesus looked at the child and spoke quietly to her.

'Come along, little girl, it's time to get up now. I think you need something to eat.'

The girl stood up, walked about and seemed to have recovered. Everyone who heard about it was amazed.

The good Samaritan

A teacher of the law asked Jesus a question one day.

'I know I must love God and love my neighbour,' he said, 'but who is my neighbour?' Jesus told this story to explain.

'A man was going on a journey from Jerusalem to Jericho. On a lonely road, robbers attacked him. They tore his clothes and beat him up, then left him at the side of the road, half dead.

'A priest came along the road a bit later. But he just walked past on the other side of the road.

'Next a Levite came along. He had a quick look, but he too hurried by on the other side of the road.

'The next person to come by was a foreigner, from nearby Samaria. When he saw the poor victim of the mugging, the Samaritan felt very sorry for him. First he cleaned and bandaged his wounds. Then he put him on his donkey and carried him to the nearest inn where he took care of him.

'The next day the Samaritan gave some money to the innkeeper. "Look after this man until he is better. If it costs any more, I'll pay you the next time I call," said the Samaritan.

'Who do you think acted like a neighbour to the wounded man?' asked Jesus.

'The one who was kind to him,' replied the teacher.

'Make sure you act in the same way to anyone, friend or enemy, who needs your help,' said Jesus.

The man who had too much

Jesus talked to a crowd of people another day about what really mattered in life.

'Life is more than the things you own,' said Jesus. 'Let me tell you a story about a rich farmer. One year he had such a huge harvest that he didn't have enough room in his barns to store it all. So he said to himself, "I'll pull down my barns and build bigger ones. I will have so much stored that I can sit back and enjoy myself."

'But that night God said to the man, "Tonight it is time for you to die. What good will all your possessions be to you now?"

'So,' said Jesus, 'be careful not to value the things you own more than the things you need to learn about God.'

The lost sheep

Another time the Pharisees from the temple criticised Jesus because he made time for people who knew they had not lived the way God wanted them to. Jesus asked the Pharisees to imagine they owned a hundred sheep.

'What would you do if you lost just one sheep? You would leave the ninety-nine sheep and look for the lost one. When you had found it you would bring it home and tell all your friends because you would be so pleased.

'In just the same way, there is more joy in heaven over one person who realises they need to say sorry to God and comes to him for forgiveness than ninety-nine good people who don't need to say sorry. God loves everyone he has made. He cares about any who wander away from him.'

33

Who is the greatest?

Jesus wanted to teach people not to think of themselves as better than others, so he told them this story.

'Two men went into the temple to pray to God.

'One, a religious leader, was very sure of himself. He stood where everyone could see him and prayed aloud, "God, I thank you that I am not greedy, or dishonest like other people. I pray a lot and give away some of my money to the poor. I'm glad I'm not like that tax collector over there."

'The other was a tax collector. He went to a corner of the temple and looked down at the floor as he prayed. All he could say was, "God, please have mercy on me for all the wrong things I have done."

'Of these two men, the tax collector was more at peace with God when he went home. He knew how wrong his life was and asked for forgiveness,' explained Jesus. 'God hears people who are humble and know they need him to help them.'

Jesus welcomes children

Wh
hile Jesus was talking to the crowd, many people were bringing their children to him to be blessed. Some of the disciples saw what was happening and were annoyed with the people.

'Don't be angry with them,' said Jesus, as he welcomed the children to him.

'But Jesus,' cried his friends, 'you have more important things to do than spend time with these children!'

'Not at all,' said Jesus. 'Let the children come to me. God's kingdom belongs to people like them. Everyone must come to God in the same way a child does, accepting and trusting him with simple faith.'

The rich young man

Ayoung man once came to Jesus and knelt before him.

'What must I do to live for ever in heaven?' he asked.

'You know the commandments that Moses taught in the scriptures. Obey those commandments.'

'I have, ever since I was young,' said the man.

Jesus then said something the man really did not want to hear.

'Go and sell all that you own. Give the money to the poor, then come and follow me.'

The young man suddenly looked very disappointed. He was rich and had many possessions. He didn't want to give them away. Jesus saw how sad the man looked. He then said something that sounded rather strange.

'It is easier for a camel to walk through the eye of a needle than for a rich man to enter God's kingdom.'

The people nearby gasped at these words.

'Then who can be saved?' they asked.

'God can make everything possible,' said Jesus.

Peter then said, 'We have left everything to follow you.'

'I know,' replied Jesus. 'Don't worry; anyone who gives up things for the sake of God's kingdom will have the special treasure he gives in heaven. Those who seem to be unimportant now will be important in God's kingdom. These people will live with God for ever.'

Learning to love

In the time of Jesus, shepherds looked after both sheep and goats in their herds. The shepherd could easily tell the two apart. Jesus explained to the people that they were a bit like sheep and goats.

'There will come a time when God will tell you how pleased he is with you. He will say, "Well done for all the times you fed me when I was hungry and gave me water when I was thirsty. Thank you for the times you looked after me when I was ill and when you visited me in prison."

'You will look puzzled and you will ask God when you did all these things for him. God will answer that every time you did anything for someone else, it was just as if you were doing it for him.

'But God won't be pleased with everyone. "I'm sorry you didn't help me or look after me when I needed it," he will say.

'These people will also not understand. They will say to God, "When were there times we didn't help you?"

'God will answer that if they didn't help someone who needed it, that was the same as not helping him. So if you want to please

God and show him that you love him, start now. Live your life in a way that helps other people and it will be just as though you are doing it for God.'

A gift for Jesus

Jesus was eating supper at the house of a man named Simon.

While he was sitting at the table, a woman came in. She carried a jar of beautiful but very expensive ointment. She went to Jesus and, breaking open the jar, she poured the ointment over his head.

The other people in the house watched. They couldn't believe what they were seeing.

'What are you doing, woman?' cried one of Jesus' friends. 'Tell her, Jesus. This ointment could have been sold for nearly a year's wages and the money given to the poor.'

'Leave her alone,' said Jesus quietly. 'You will always have the poor with you. You can help them at any time. I will not always be with you. This woman has prepared my body for burial.'

Jesus knew that the time was soon coming when he would be arrested by his enemies and then put to death.

His friends still didn't understand that he would be taken away from them.

Blind Bartimaeus sees

Jesus was passing through Jericho on his way to Jerusalem. He walked with his friends, followed by a large crowd of people.

Beside the road sat Bartimaeus. He was blind and had to beg to get money so he could eat. As the crowd moved out of the city the blind man heard that Jesus was there and called out to him.

'Jesus, Son of David, please help me! Have mercy on me!'

'Hush! Be quiet!' said people in the crowd. 'He doesn't want to be bothered by you.'

This made Bartimaeus cry out even more loudly! He was not going to be put off.

'Jesus, Son of David, help me!' he cried again.

Through the noise of the crowd Jesus heard him and stopped.

'Call that man over to me,' he said.

'It's all right, Bartimaeus. He wants you to go to him,' the crowd urged. 'Hurry, he won't wait for ever!'

At this, Bartimaeus threw off his cloak and stumbled his way over to Jesus.

'What do you want me to do?' asked Jesus.

'Master, please let me see,' begged Bartimaeus.

'Go on your way,' said Jesus. 'You have been made well because of your faith.'

Then suddenly Bartimaeus could see. He was so overjoyed he danced about all over the place.

'Thank you, Jesus! Thank you, God!' he shouted as he followed Jesus along with the crowd.

Jesus meets Zacchaeus

Huge numbers of people had come out to see Jesus while he was in Jericho. One man in particular wanted to take a look at him. He was a rich tax collector named Zacchaeus.

Zacchaeus was very short and couldn't see over the people in front of him. So he ran ahead and climbed into the low spreading branches of a fig tree so he could get a better view. When he reached the place, Jesus seemed to know already that Zacchaeus was there. He looked up through the dappled shade of the leaves.

'Zacchaeus!' Jesus called. 'Come down here. I would like to come to your house today.'

Surprised though he was, Zacchaeus jumped down and

welcomed Jesus into his house.

Now Zacchaeus was rich because he often cheated people when he collected their taxes. Many of the crowd muttered about the fact that Jesus was going to eat with a man who cheated other people. But Zacchaeus was changed by his meeting with Jesus.

'Jesus,' declared Zacchaeus, 'I'm going to give half of what I own to the poor in the town. And if I have cheated anyone, I will repay four times what I owe them.'

'Well done, Zacchaeus!' cried Jesus, loudly enough for everyone to hear. 'This is the reason I came to live among you, to look for and save people like you whose lives need to be changed.'

Lazarus is brought back to life

Lazarus, one of Jesus' friends, was very ill. Lazarus' sisters, Mary and Martha, were very anxious, and sent a message to Jesus to tell him about their brother.

Jesus heard the message but knew God wanted him to stay where he was because a great miracle was going to happen.

Lazarus did not get better. He died and was buried in a tomb. It was four days before Jesus reached Bethany where it happened.

Lazarus' sister Mary was so upset she sat at home crying. But Martha ran out to meet Jesus.

'If you had been here my brother wouldn't have died,' she said. 'But even now I know that whatever you ask God to do, it will happen.'

'Your brother will live again,' said Jesus.

'I know he will one day,' replied Martha.

But Jesus said, 'I am life itself and anyone who trusts me will know real life and will never die. Do you believe this?'

'I do,' said Martha. 'You are Jesus, God's Son, the one we have been waiting for.'

Then Martha fetched her sister. Mary came from

the house and there was a great crowd with her, all weeping for Lazarus. Even Jesus cried for his friend.

'Open up the tomb,' commanded Jesus.

The people were horrified. The body of Lazarus would smell terrible after four days. But they did as Jesus asked and were amazed at what they saw.

Lazarus walked out of the tomb. He was alive!

Many people saw and believed in Jesus after the great miracle of Lazarus coming back from death. They went to tell the Pharisees what they had seen.

Jesus rides into Jerusalem

Jesus knew it was time for him to go to Jerusalem. As he and his friends came to a village at the Mount of Olives, just outside the city, Jesus called two of them to him.

'Go over to the village. You will find there the foal of a donkey tied up outside a door. Untie it and bring it to me.'

'What if the owner asks what we are doing?' asked one of them.

'If that happens, just tell him that the master needs it,' said Jesus.

The two men did as Jesus had instructed them. Then they spread some clothes over the foal's back to make a kind of saddle. Jesus climbed up and they set off into the city of Jerusalem.

The people had heard that Jesus was on his way and crowded the streets. Some threw their cloaks on the ground in front of him. Some cut branches off the palm trees and waved them about. Everyone was shouting.

'Here comes the promised king! Hooray for Jesus! At last he's here!'

They were all very excited to see Jesus.

The poor widow

When Jesus reached the temple area, he watched the people give money towards its work. Rich people came and put large amounts into the treasury.

But Jesus drew the attention of his friends to a poor widow. Reaching into her purse she pulled out the only money she had. She dropped just two small coins into one of the thirteen collecting boxes.

'This woman has put in more than any of the others today,' he said. 'The rich people gave a little of the huge amount they have. But she has given everything she owned.'

The Passover meal

After riding the foal into the city, Jesus spent nearly a week teaching the people in Jerusalem. He upset the leaders of the temple by explaining that many of the things they were doing were not right. They started plotting to get rid of him. Judas, one of his twelve disciples, had already planned with them a way to betray him.

When the time came to celebrate the Passover meal, Jesus called his disciples together in an upstairs room. Then he put a towel around his waist, took a bowl of water and washed the feet of each of his friends. As this was normally done by the servants, Peter became upset.

'You shouldn't be washing my feet,' Peter exclaimed.

'Rather I should be washing yours!'

'You'll understand this later,' said Jesus. 'Now you have seen me do this for you, you must learn to love and care for each other in the same way.'

After that, at the table, Jesus blessed the bread and broke it into pieces. He handed some to each of them.

'This is my body,' he said. 'Each time you eat bread like this, remember me.'

Then he took the cup of wine. He blessed this also and handed it round for each of them to drink.

'This is my blood,' he said. 'Each time you drink like this, remember me.'

He showed them that the bread and wine were always there to remind them of his death for them.

The kiss of betrayal

After they had eaten together, Jesus led the disciples to a garden called Gethsemane. It was late and the disciples were tired. Jesus knew that he would soon be arrested, tried and

52

killed. There wasn't much time left. He took three of his closest friends with him away from the others.

'Stay here and watch with me while I pray to my Father in heaven,' he said. Jesus went away from them a little and prayed.

'Father, if there is any way you want to stop all this, please do it now. But if this is really what must happen, I am ready.'

When he returned, his three friends had fallen asleep. He woke them and twice more asked them to watch while he prayed. Each time he came back he found them asleep. Jesus was very sad.

'Couldn't you keep awake just this little while?' he asked.

By that time the soldiers were coming to the garden to arrest him. Their torches flared in the darkness. With them came Judas. He whispered to one of the soldiers.

'The man I kiss on the cheek is the one you are to arrest,' he said.

Judas stepped up to Jesus and kissed him. Then the soldiers charged forwards and dragged Jesus away to be tried.

Jesus on trial

The Roman governor, Pontius Pilate, found it difficult to talk with Jesus. Jesus wouldn't argue with him.

Finally Pilate had had enough.

'The people say that you are the King of the Jews. Is that correct?' asked Pilate.

Jesus turned to him and replied, 'You have said it.'

Pilate didn't quite know what to do next. He took Jesus outside and showed him to the people.

'I find this man has done nothing wrong. It is the custom at this time of year to release one prisoner,' he cried. 'Who would you have me release today – Jesus, or the robber Barabbas?'

The crowd had been stirred into a frenzy by the temple leaders.

'Barabbas!' they shouted.

'Then what shall I do with Jesus?' asked Pilate.

The answer came back even louder than before. 'Crucify him!'

When he saw how wild the crowd had become, Pilate was even more worried. He took Jesus

indoors and had him whipped. The soldiers plaited thorns into a crown to put on his head. They put a purple robe on him and mocked him.

'Hail, King of the Jews!' they cried, then slapped him.

Pilate took Jesus outside and said to the people, 'This man has committed no crime.'

He had a bowl of water brought out to him and showed the people as he washed his hands.

'This death is nothing to do with me,' he said, and handed Jesus over to the Jewish leaders.

55

Jesus is crucified

Jesus was led out into the streets. He was made to carry the wood on which he would be crucified, but he stumbled and nearly fell. So the soldiers dragged a man called Simon from the crowd and made him carry it instead.

The soldiers marched Jesus to a hill called Golgotha. It was a miserable place that looked like a skull. They stripped him of his outer clothes, then nailed him to the wood, and hoisted it up to make the cross. It was a horrible punishment.

On the cross Pilate put a special sign. It read, 'This is the King of the Jews.'

There were two criminals crucified there as well, one on each side. One of them shouted to Jesus.

'You saved others from death. Why can't you save yourself and us, too?'

The other criminal was angry.

'Don't say that,' he called. 'At least we are here because we have done wrong. This man is innocent.' Then he spoke to Jesus. 'Remember me when you get to heaven.'

Jesus replied, saying, 'Today you will be with me in paradise.'

Then the sky became very dark as if there were going to be a great thunderstorm. It lasted three hours.

Then Jesus cried out in a loud voice:
'It is finished!' and then he died.

John, one of Jesus' disciples, was there comforting Mary, his mother. The other women wept when they saw what had happened to Jesus.

The empty tomb

On the Sunday morning Mary Magdalene took spices and went to visit the tomb where Jesus had been laid.

But when she arrived the stone had been rolled away from the entrance. The tomb was empty!

Through tear-stained eyes Mary Magdalene peered inside the tomb. To her amazement she saw two angels.

'Why are you weeping?' asked one of the angels.

'They have taken away the body of Jesus and I don't know where he is,' she replied. Just then she sensed a movement behind her. She turned round and saw a man. Her sight was blurred by her tears and the early morning sun.

'Sir,' she said, 'if you have taken him away, please tell me where you have put him.'

'Mary,' Jesus said quietly.

Straight away Mary recognised Jesus' voice. He was alive!

She went to hug him but he said to her, 'Do not hold me. Go to the others and tell them what you have seen.'

So she ran back with great joy, and told the disciples all that had happened.

58

Thomas believes

The disciples listened to everything Mary told them. Then that evening, even though the doors were locked, Jesus appeared in the room where they were staying. He talked for a while before leaving them. Now Thomas was not with the others when this happened. They told him about the visit but he would not believe them.

'I'll only believe it if I see Jesus for myself,' he said.

About a week later Jesus appeared again just as before. This time Thomas was there.

'So, Thomas,' said Jesus, 'touch the marks where the nails went in.' Thomas fell to his knees.

'It is you, Lord.'

'You believe because you have seen me, Thomas. Many more will believe even though they have not seen me. They will be blessed.'

Breakfast by the lake

A little while later Jesus appeared again. This time it was after the disciples had gone back to their village by the lake.

Several of the disciples were fishermen

and they had been out all night with their nets. They had caught nothing. Just as they were thinking of sailing back in, they saw a figure standing on the shore.

'Let down your nets on the other side of the boat,' the man called out.

The fishermen did as he said. They caught so many fish they had difficulty hauling in the net.

One of them called out, 'It's Jesus!'

At that, Simon Peter jumped into the water and waded ashore. The others pulled the net in and landed the catch. When they came to the beach they found Jesus there. He had a fire going already and some fish cooking. They sat with him and he gave them bread and fish to eat.

This was the last time Jesus appeared to the disciples before he went to be with his Father in heaven.

Where to find the stories in the Bible